Be An Expert With These Tips To Drawing Cartoon Faces

Drawing Expressive Cartoon Faces Tips and Techniques

Cartoon Faces

By: Gala Publication

Published By:

Gala Publication

ISBN-13: **978-1522708179**
ISBN-10: **1522708170**

©Copyright 2015 – Gala Publication

INDEX

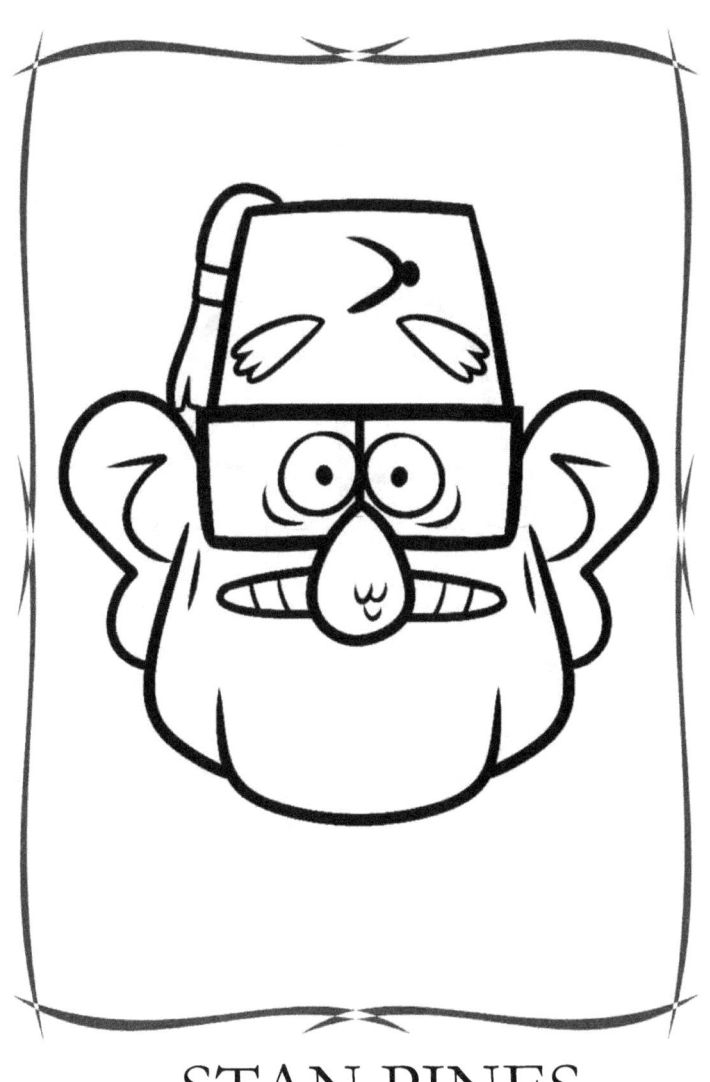

STAN PINES

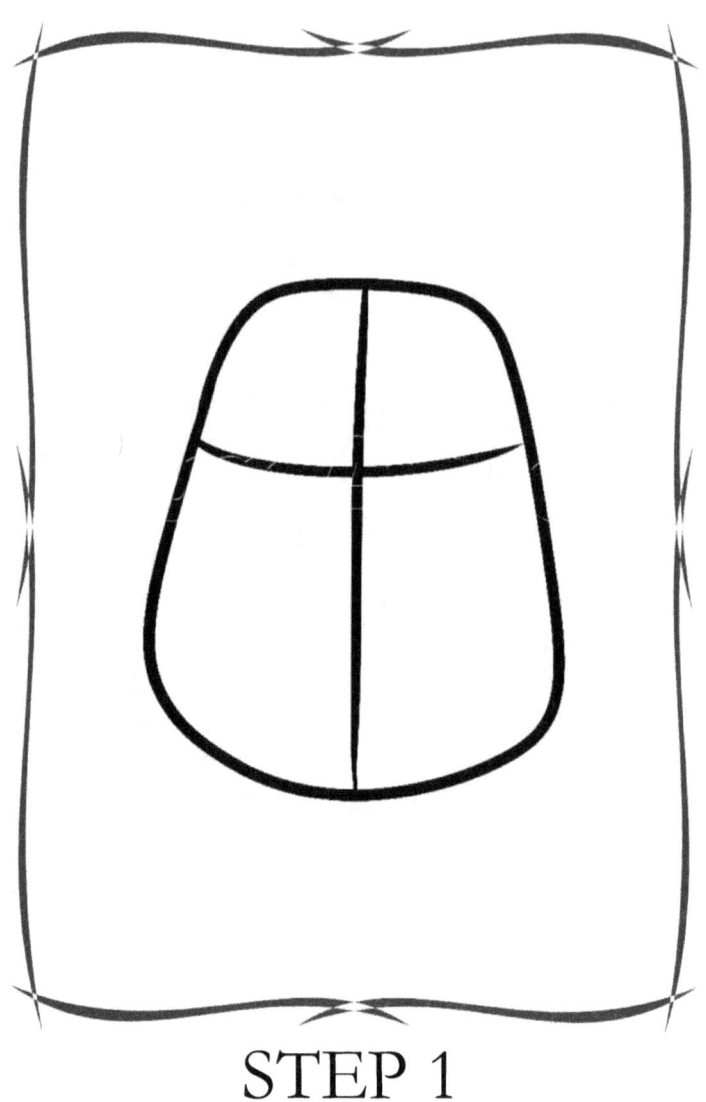

STEP 1

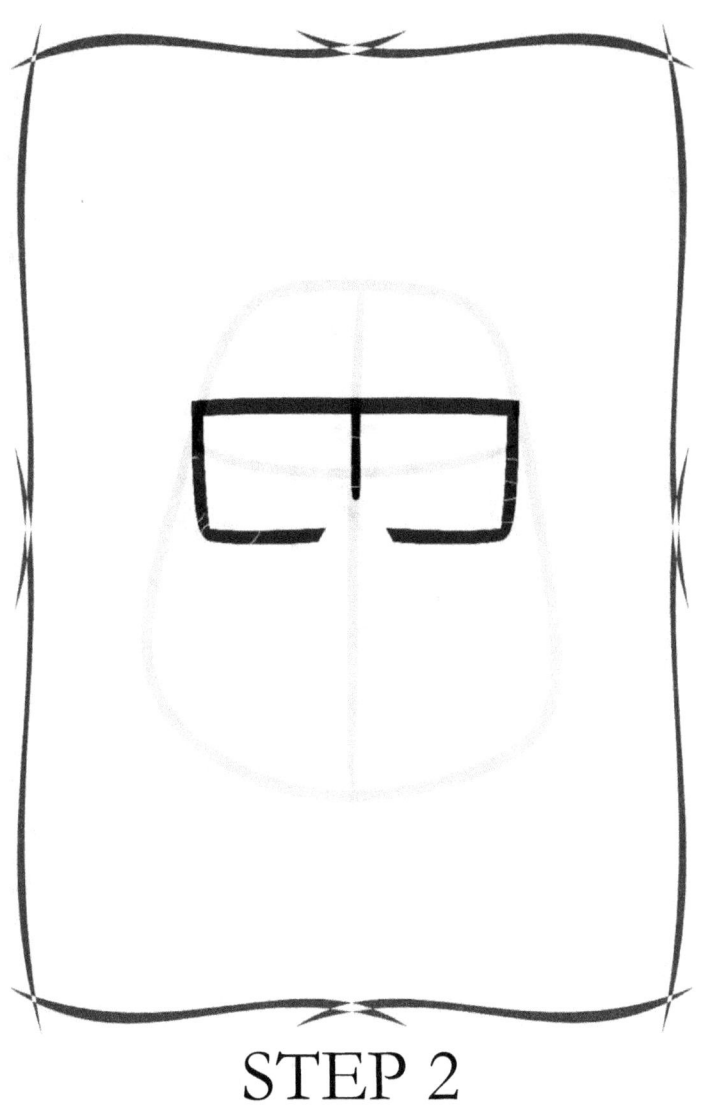

STEP 2

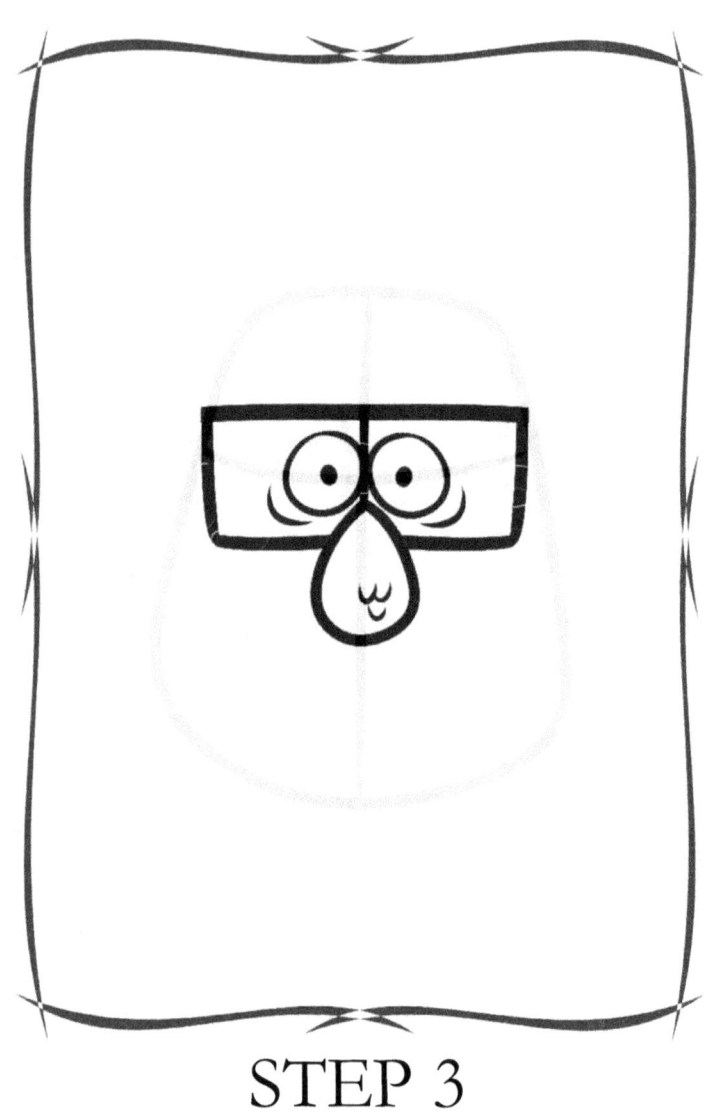

STEP 3

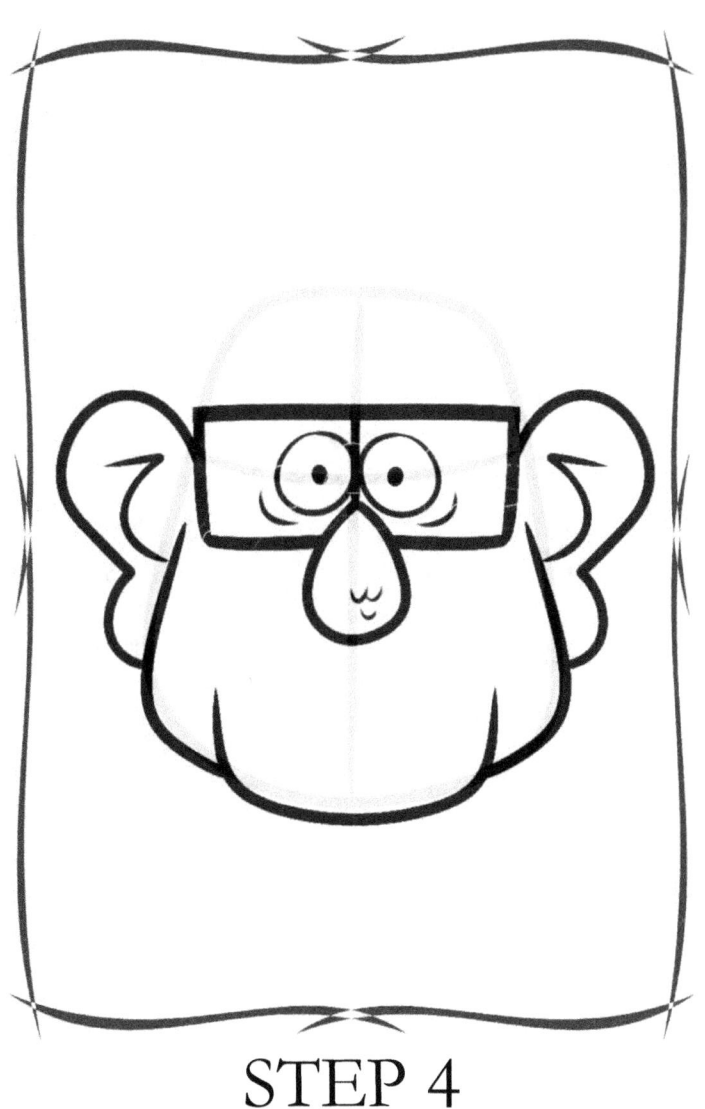

STEP 4

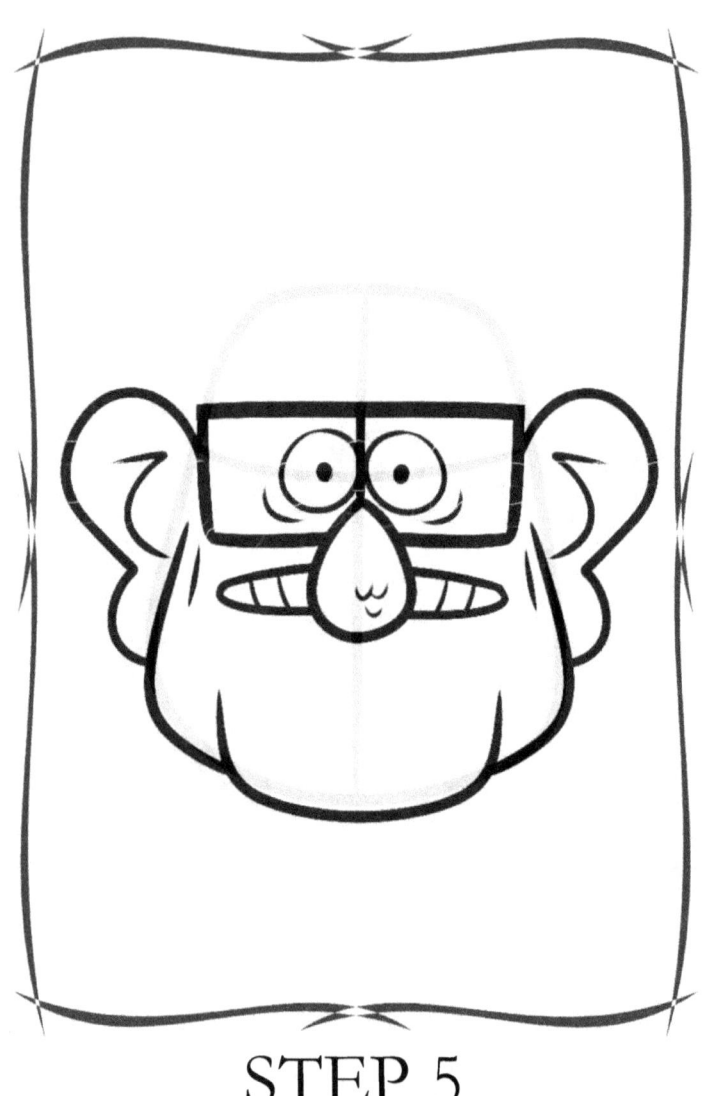

STEP 5

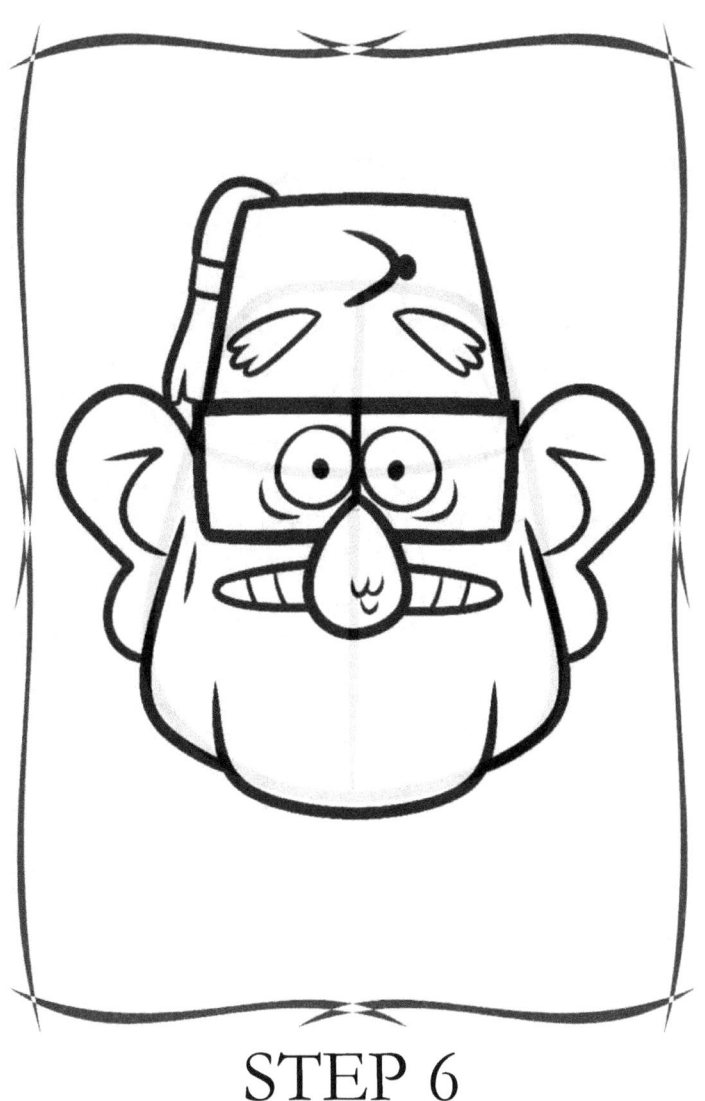

STEP 6

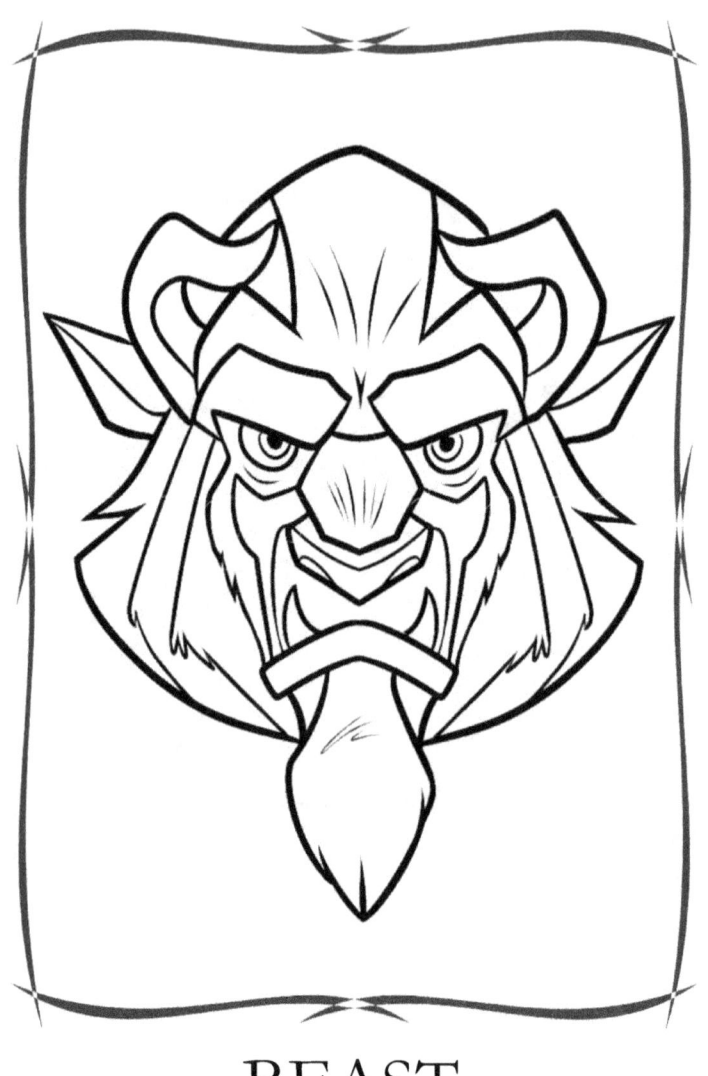

BEAST

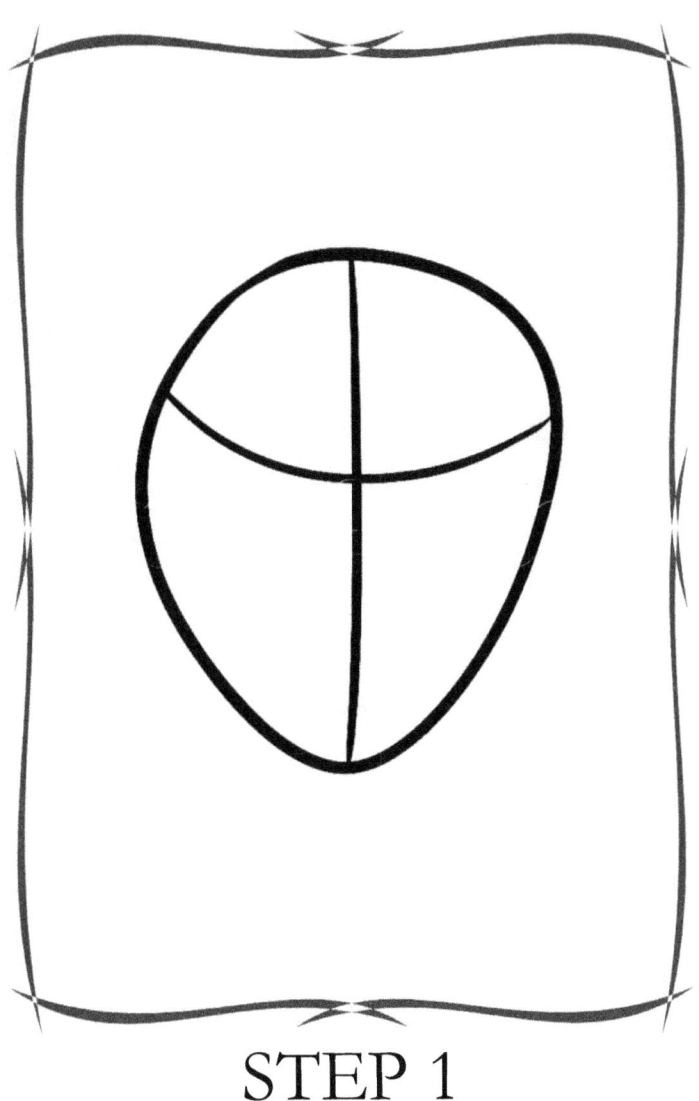

STEP 1

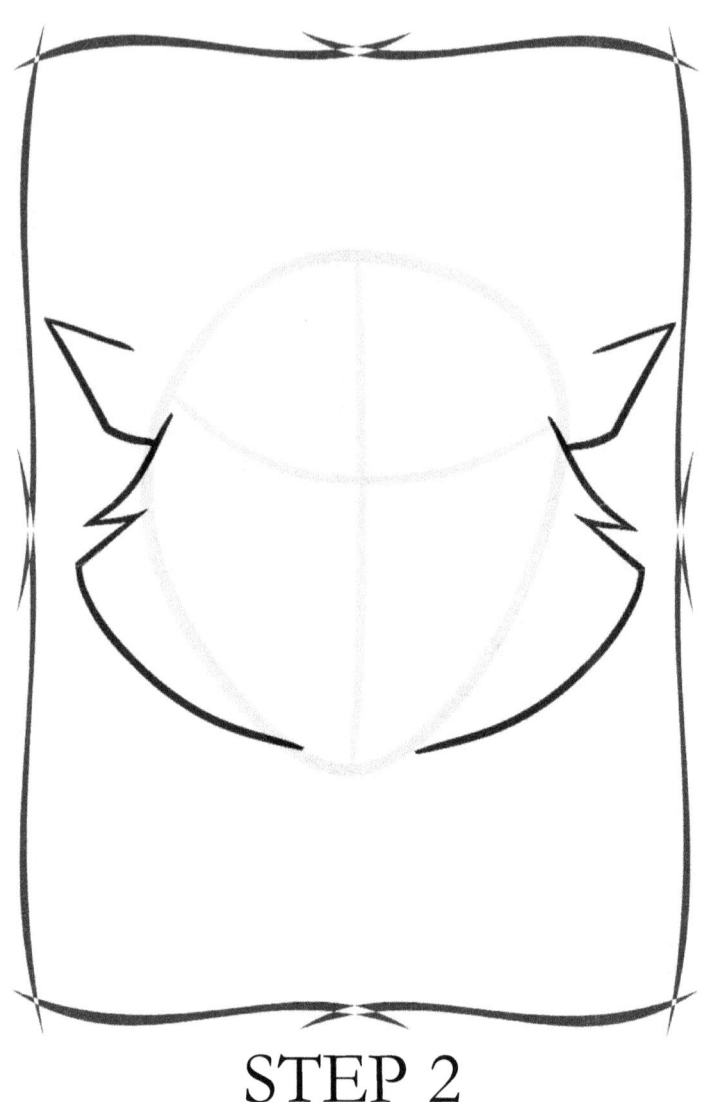

STEP 2

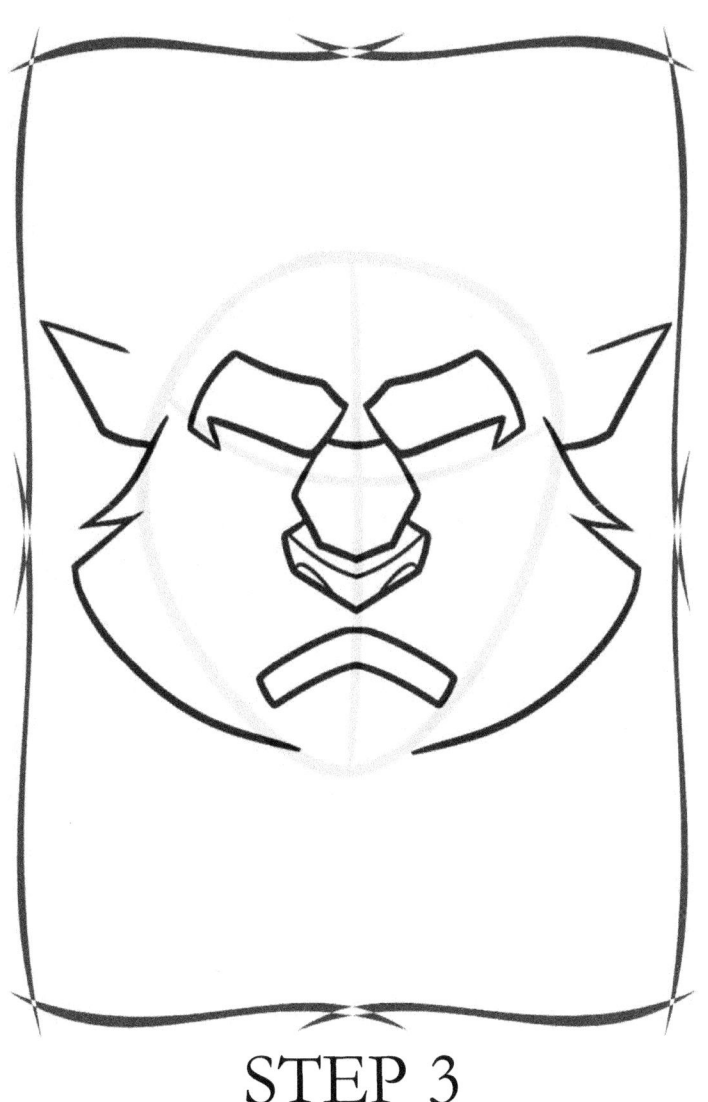

STEP 3

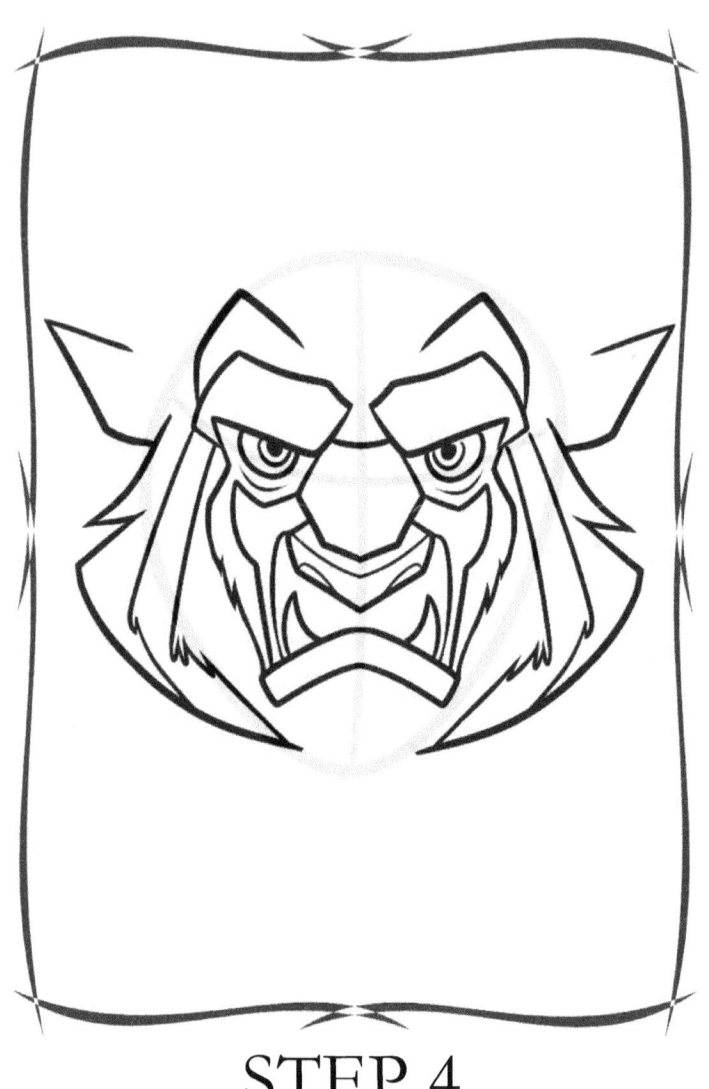

STEP 4

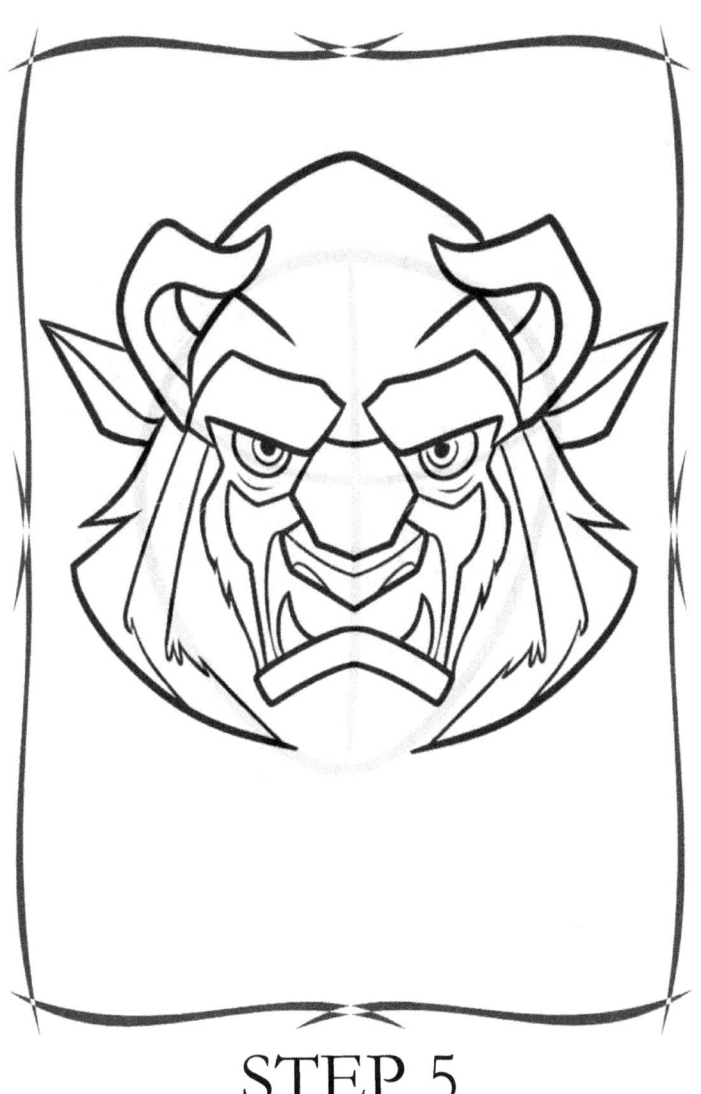

STEP 5

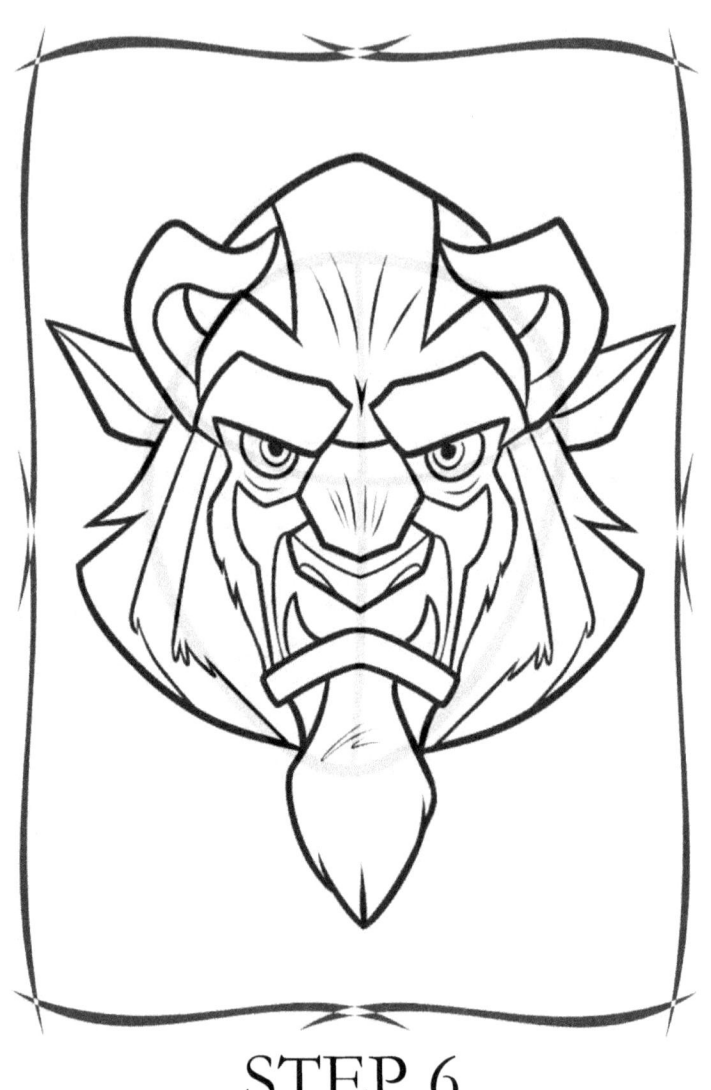

STEP 6

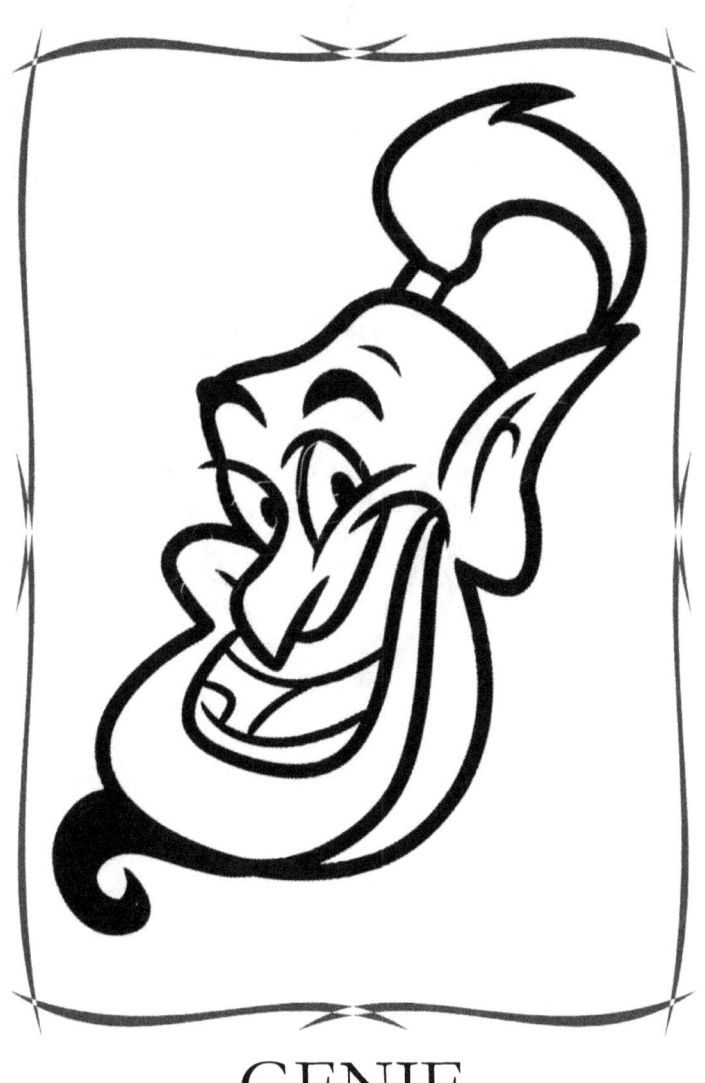

GENIE

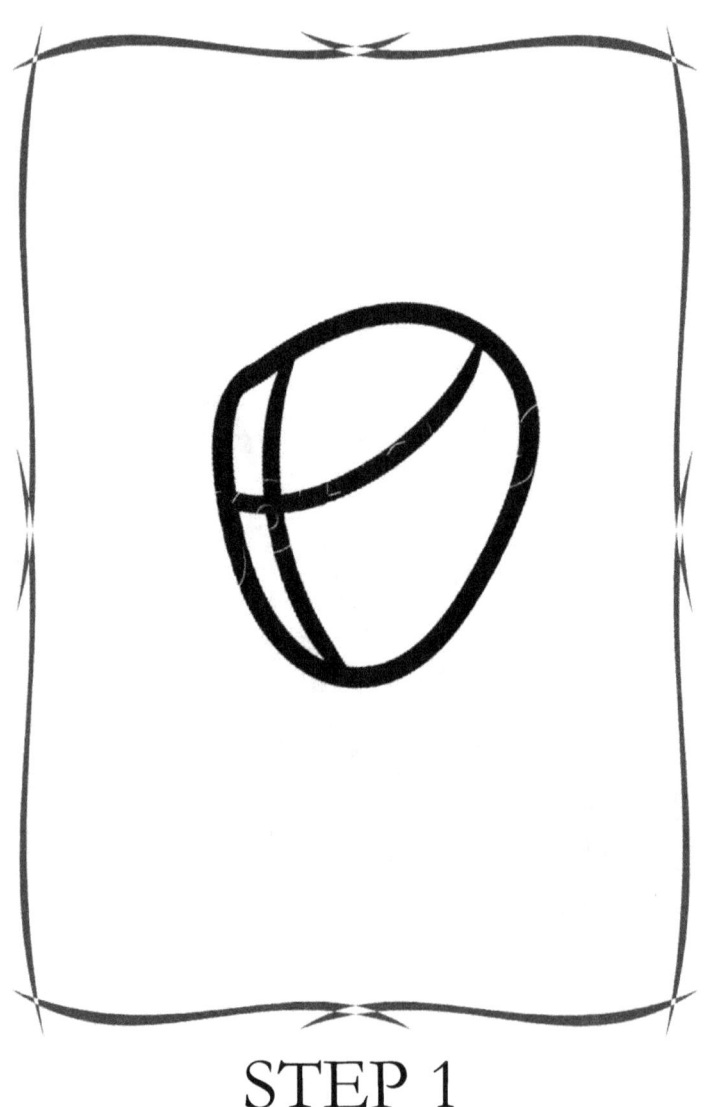

STEP 1

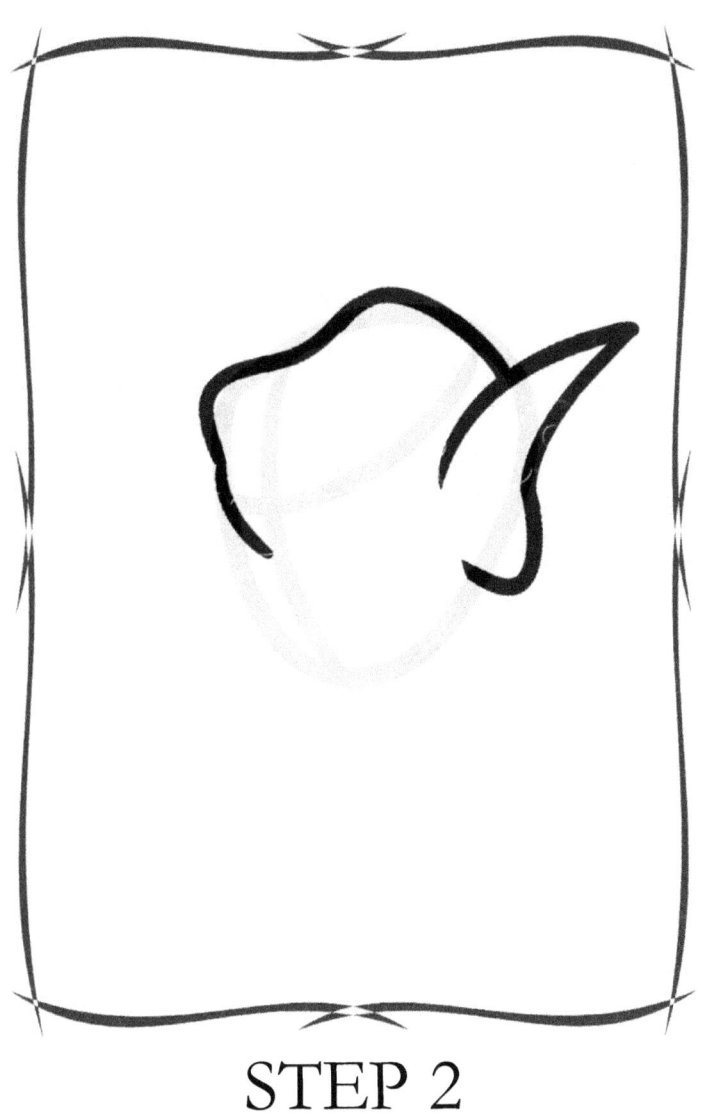

STEP 2

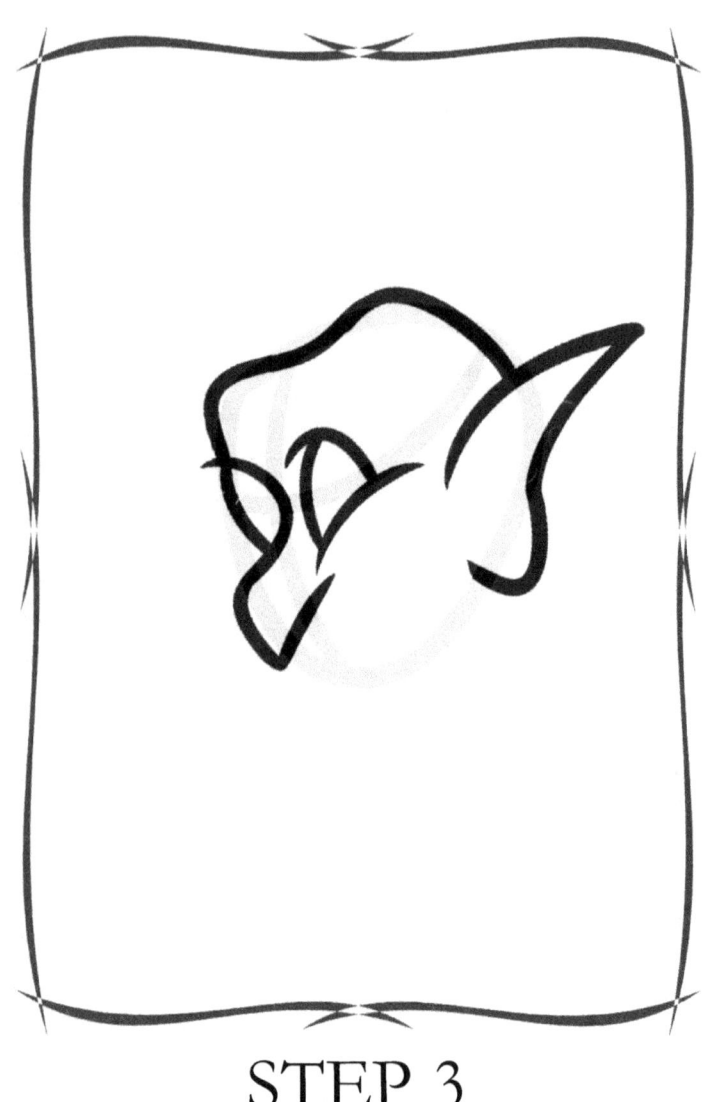

STEP 3

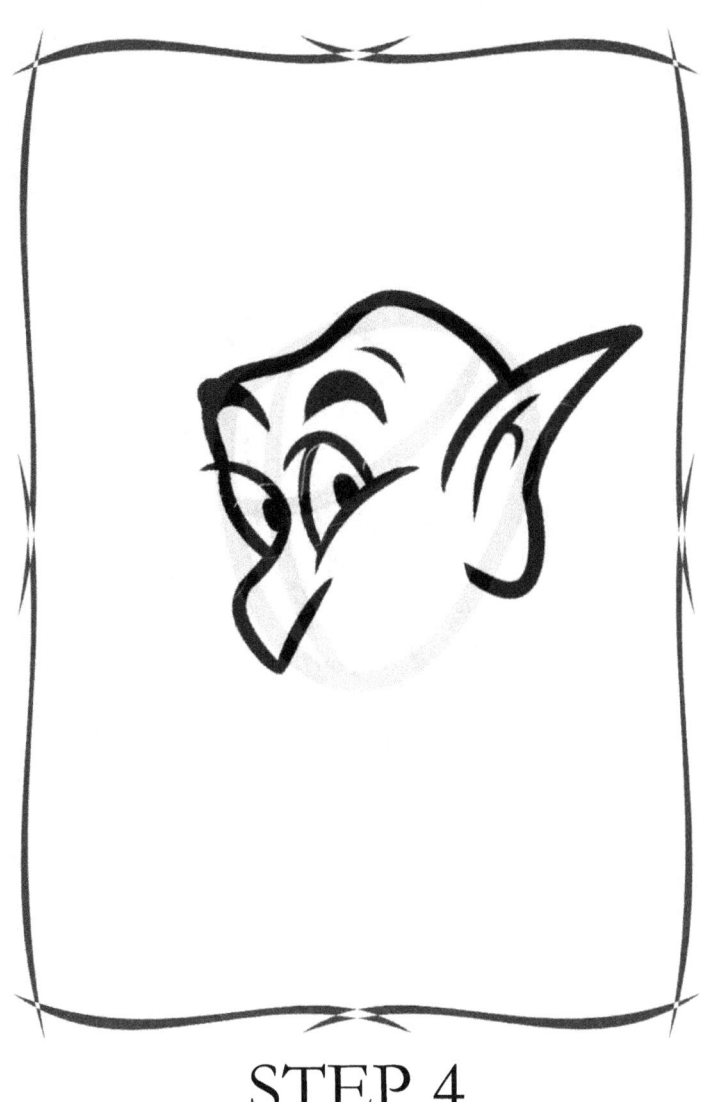

STEP 4

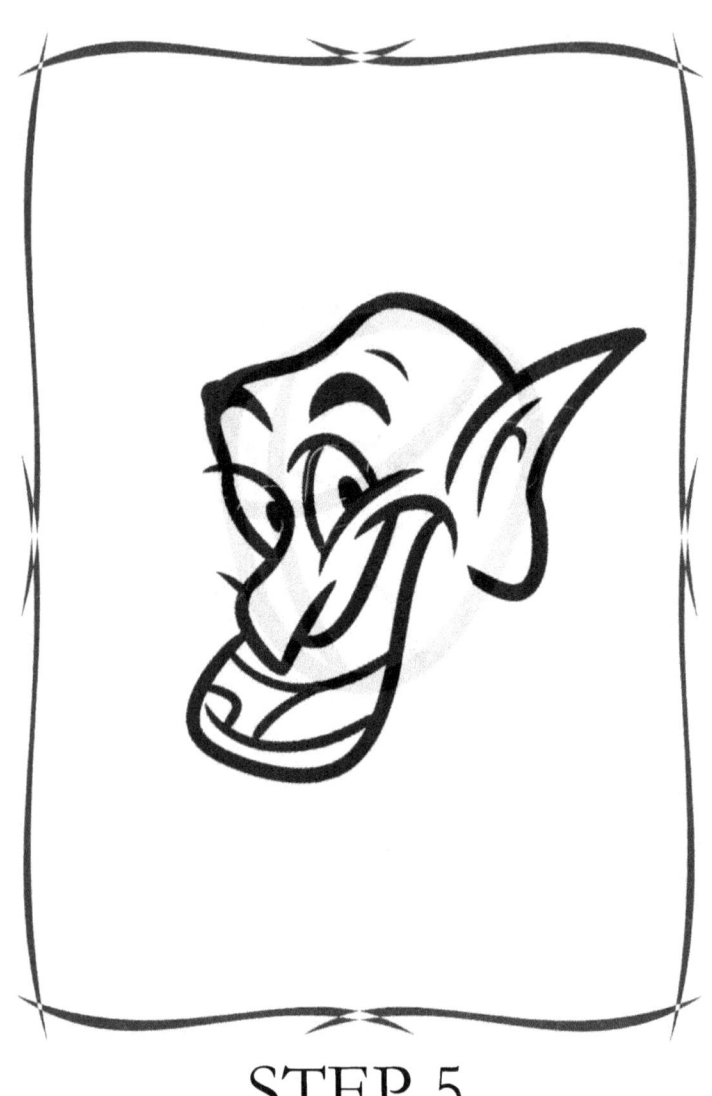

STEP 5

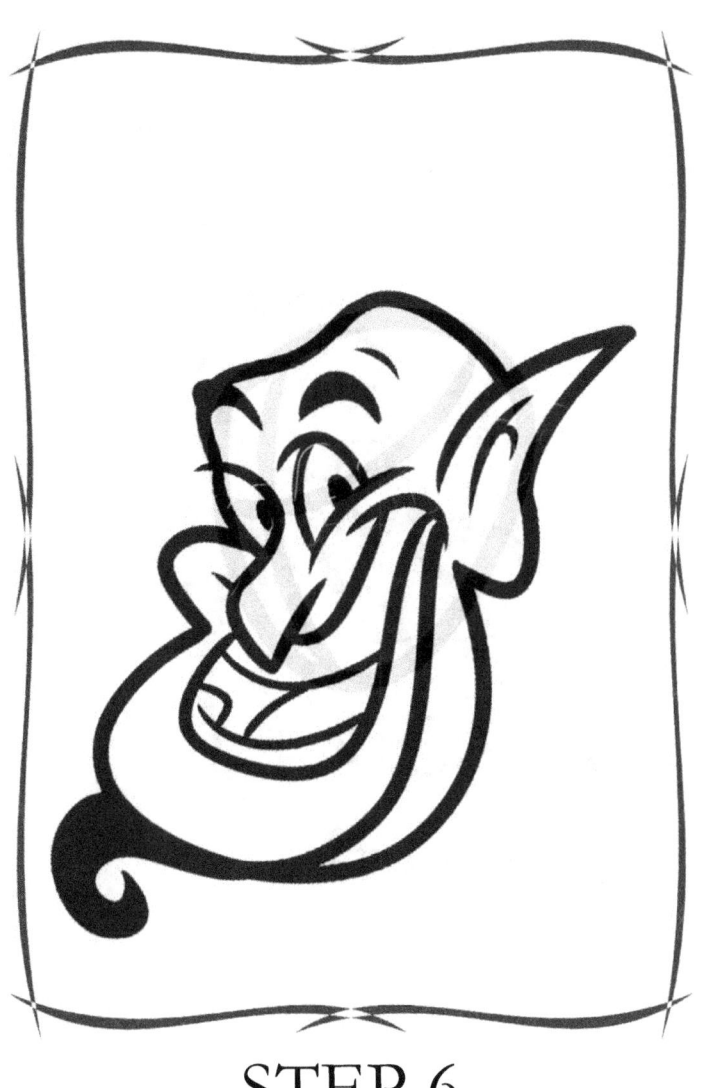

STEP 6

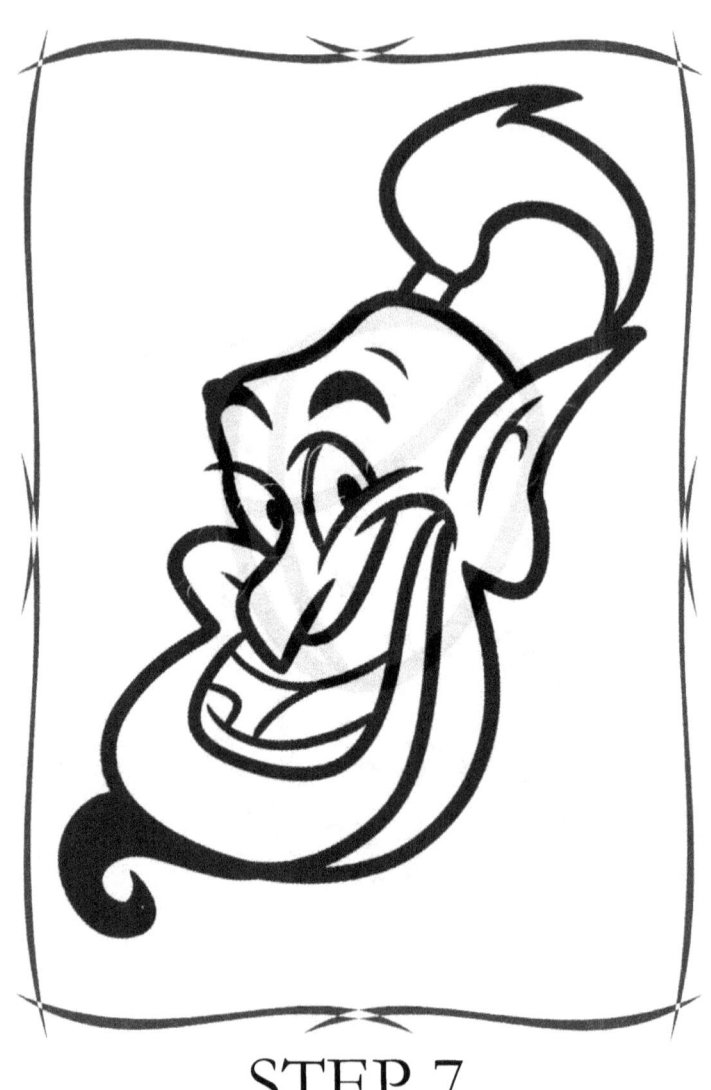

STEP 7

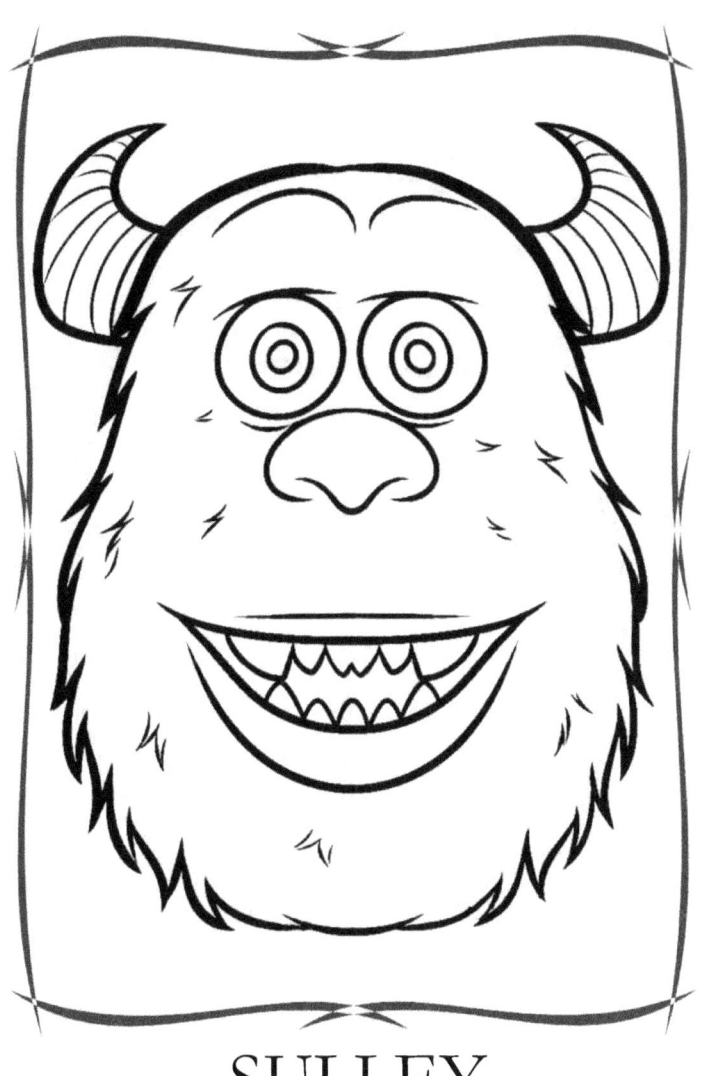

SULLEY

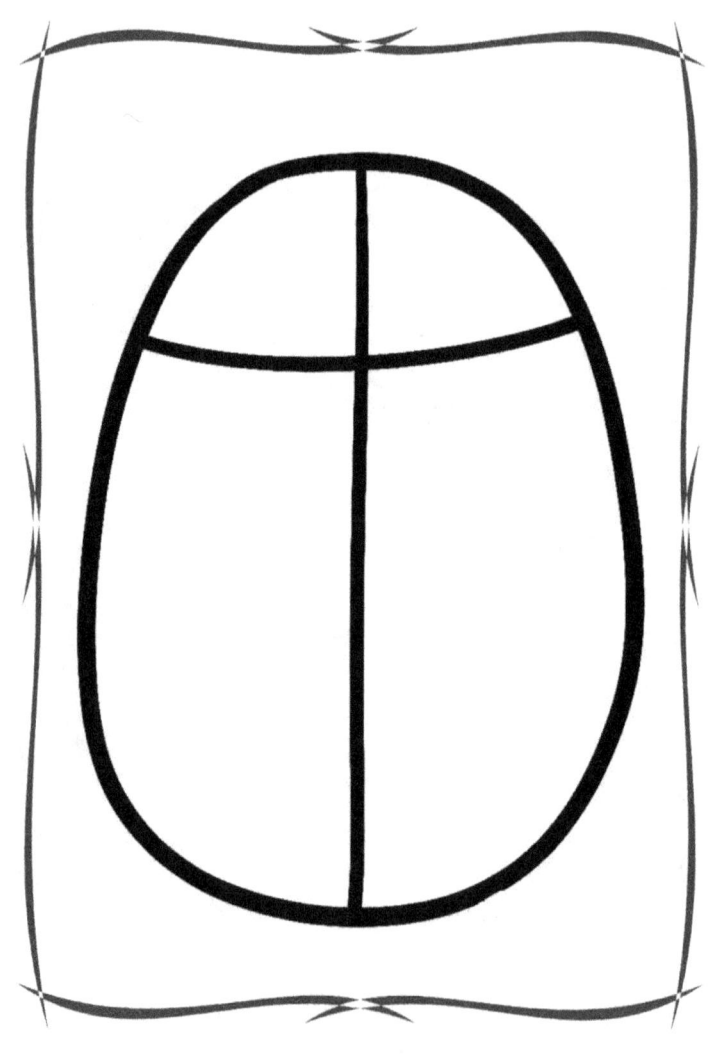

STEP 1

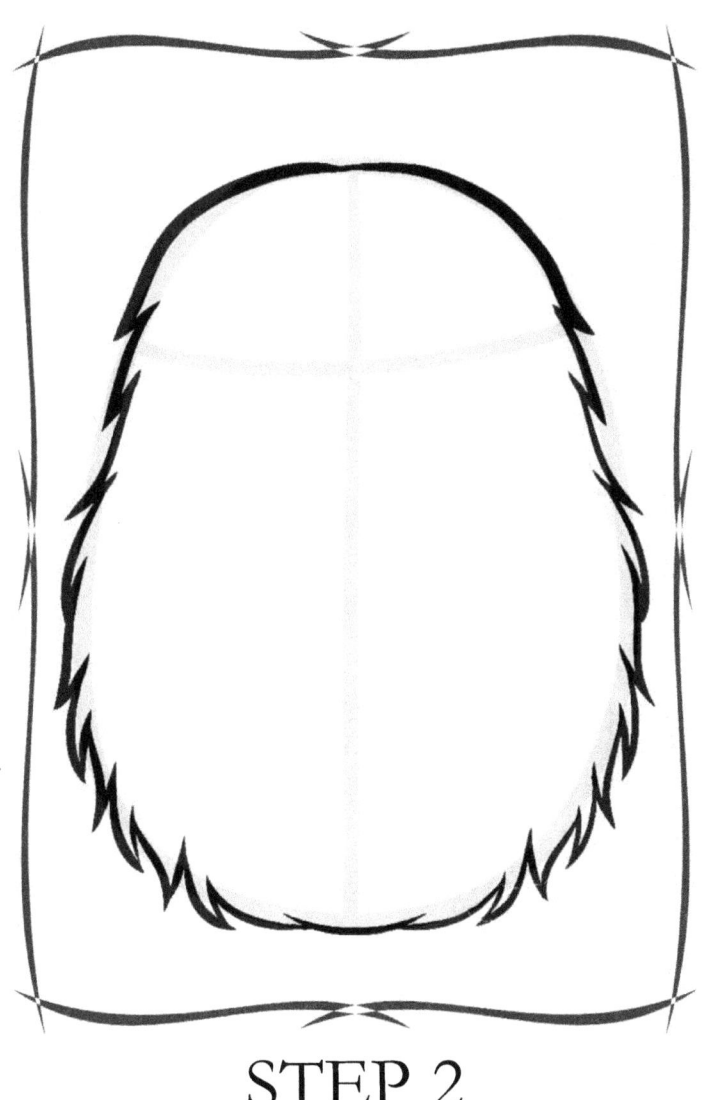

STEP 2

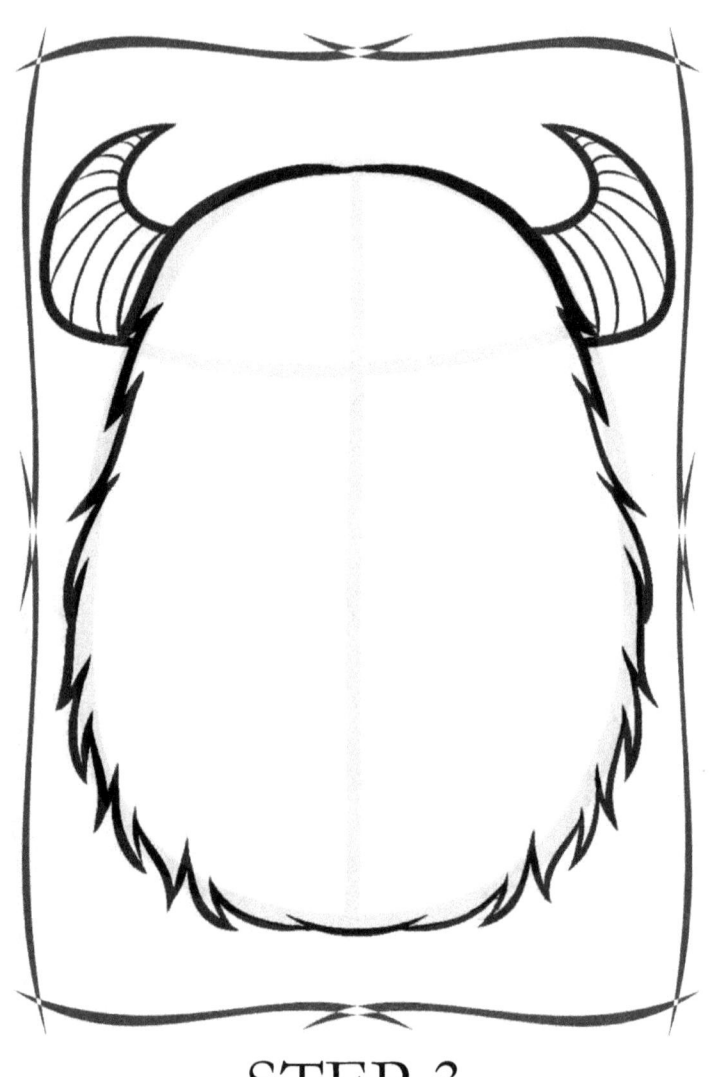

STEP 3

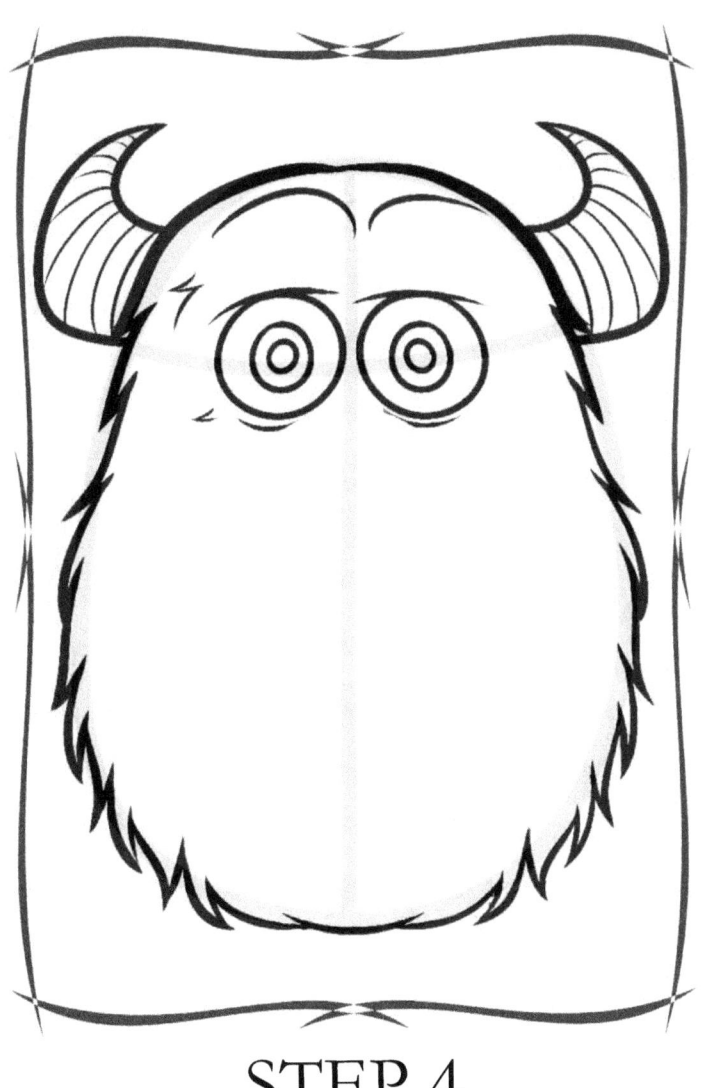

STEP 4

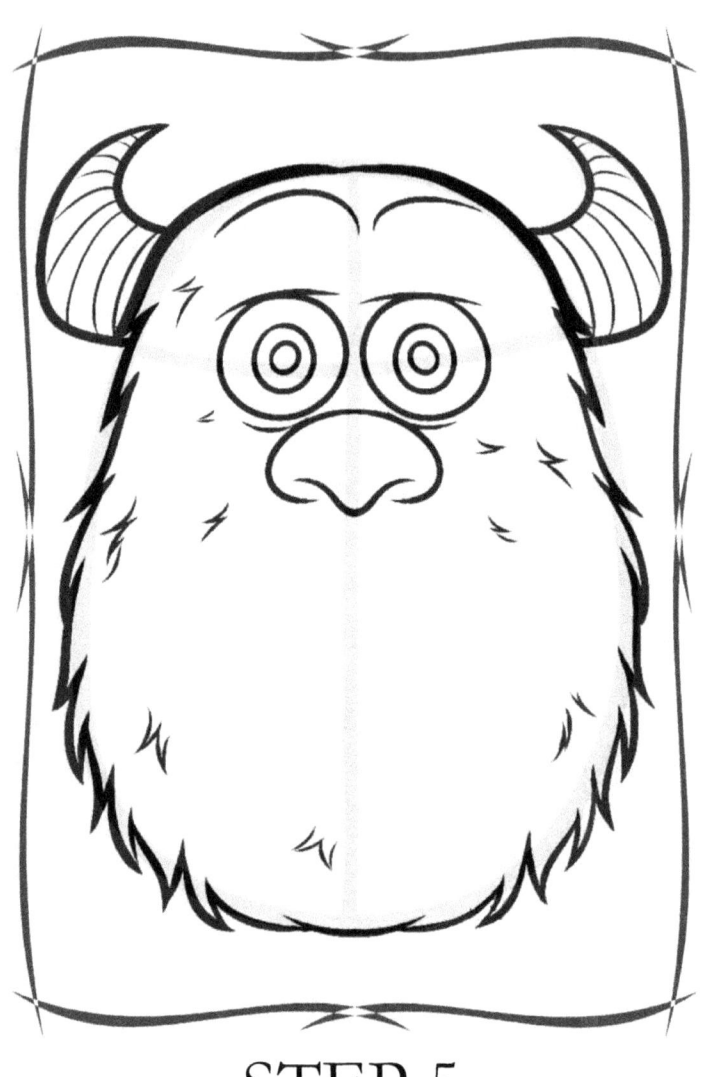

STEP 5

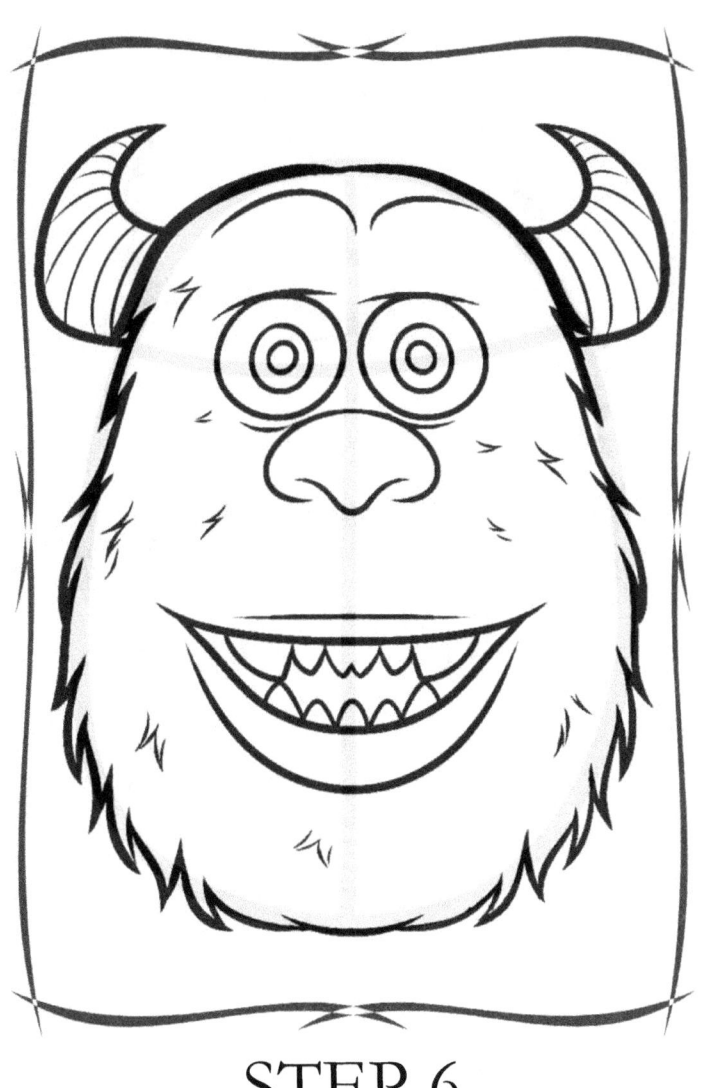

STEP 6

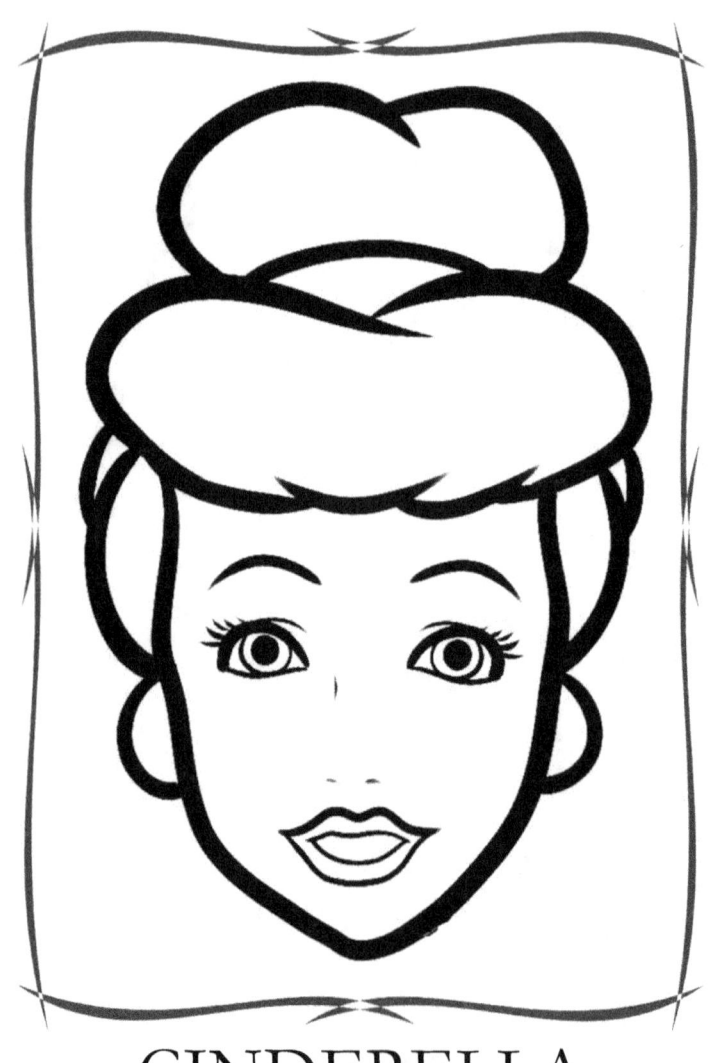

CINDERELLA

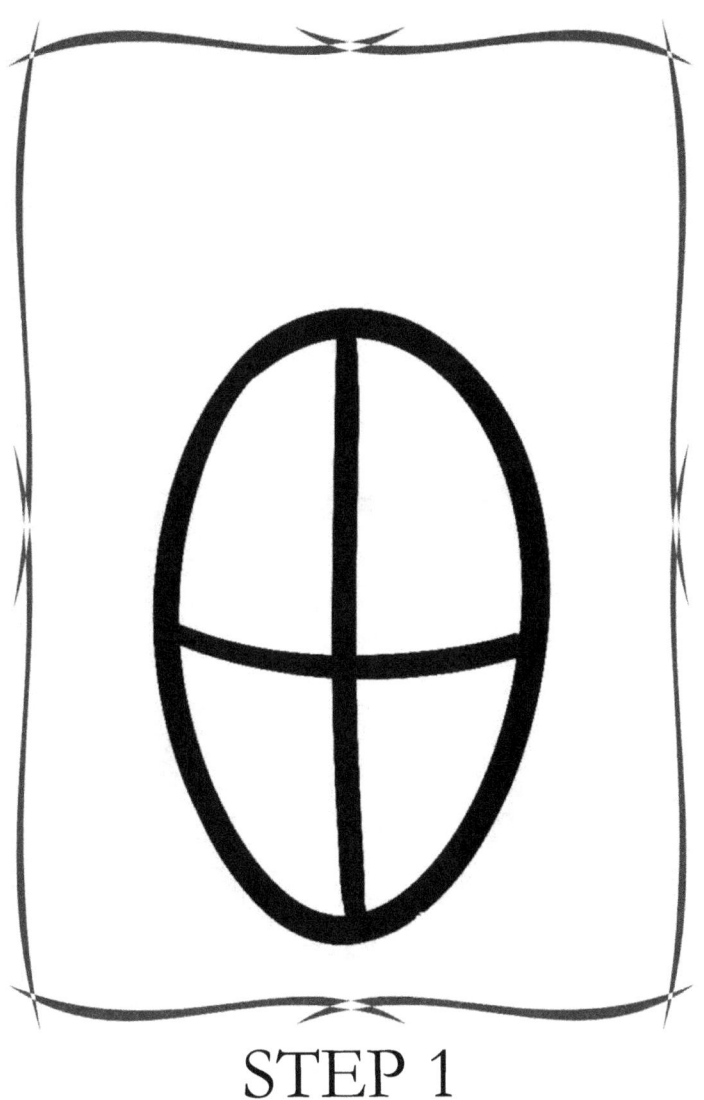

STEP 1

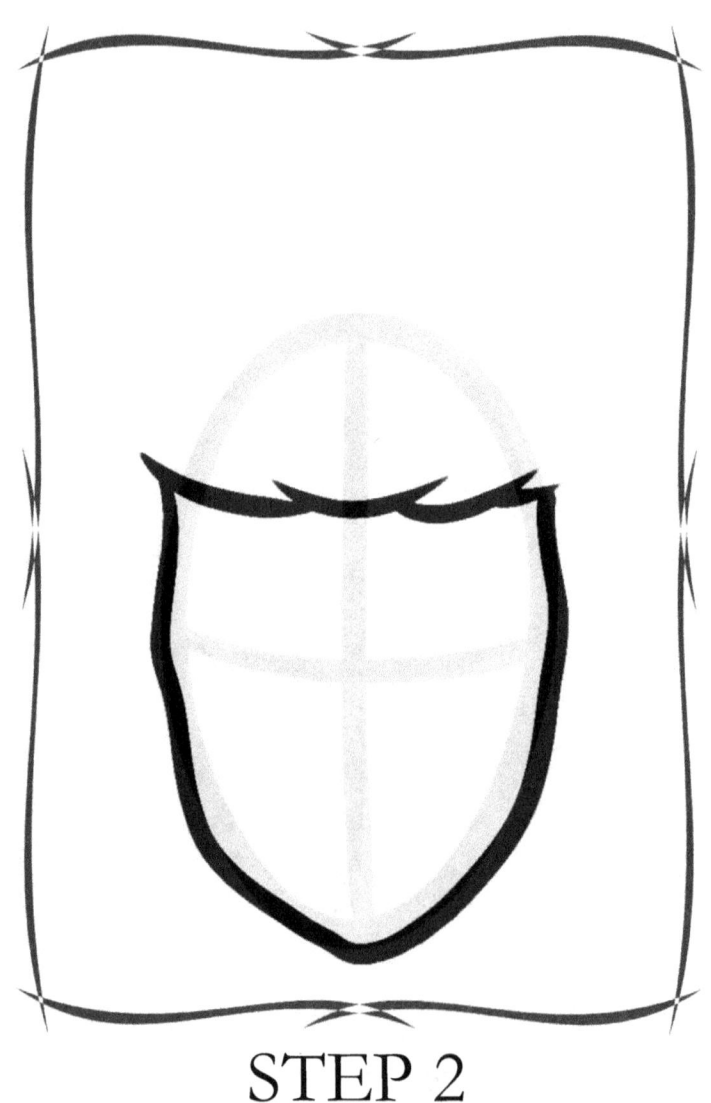

STEP 2

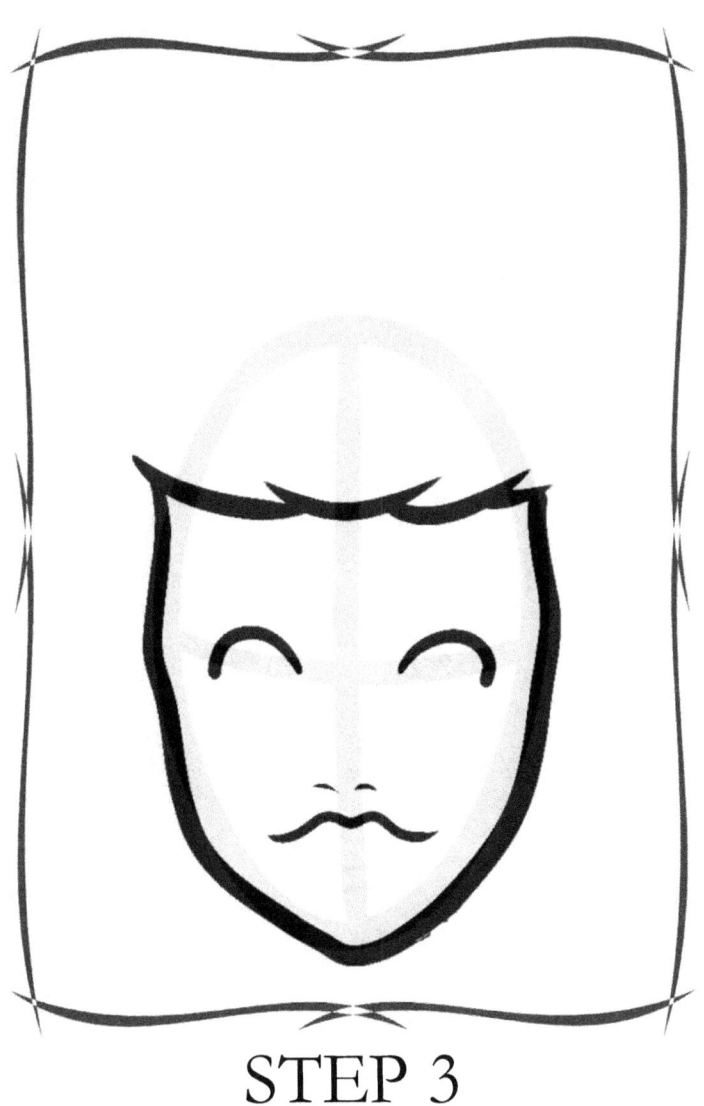

STEP 3

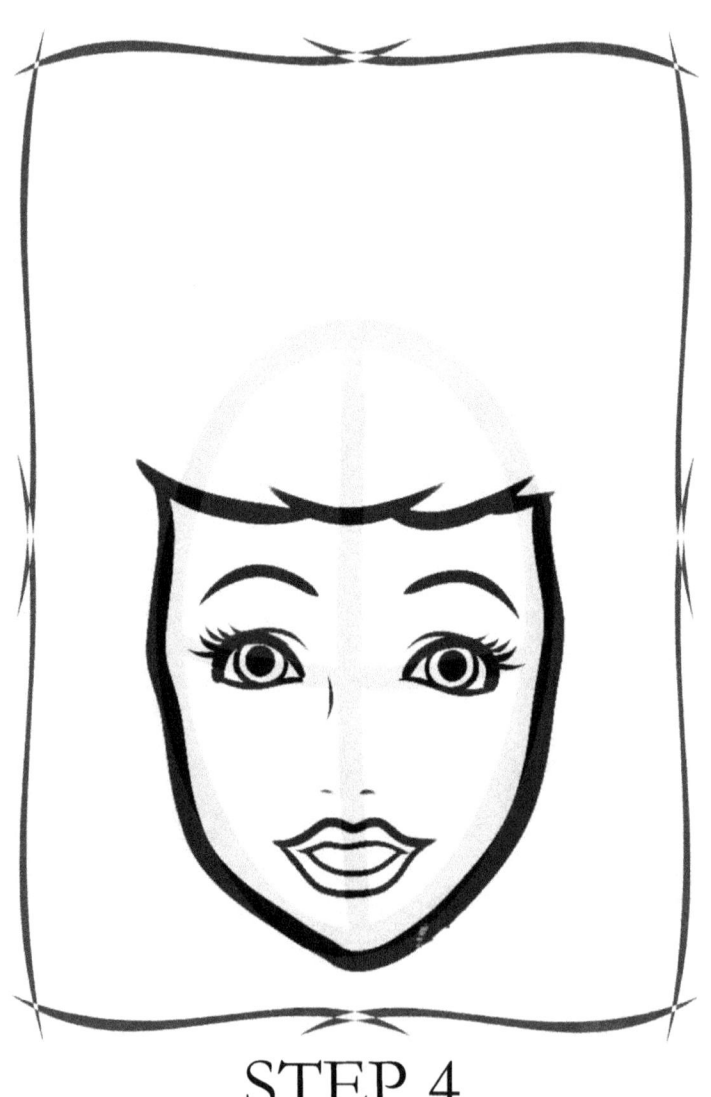

STEP 4

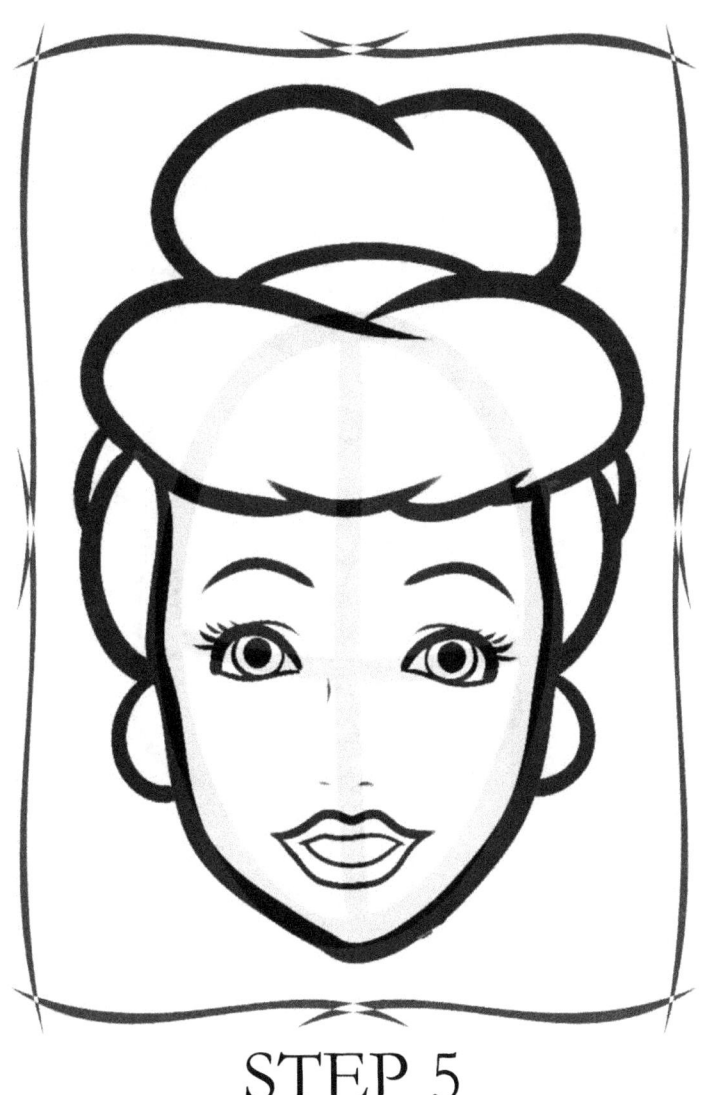

STEP 5

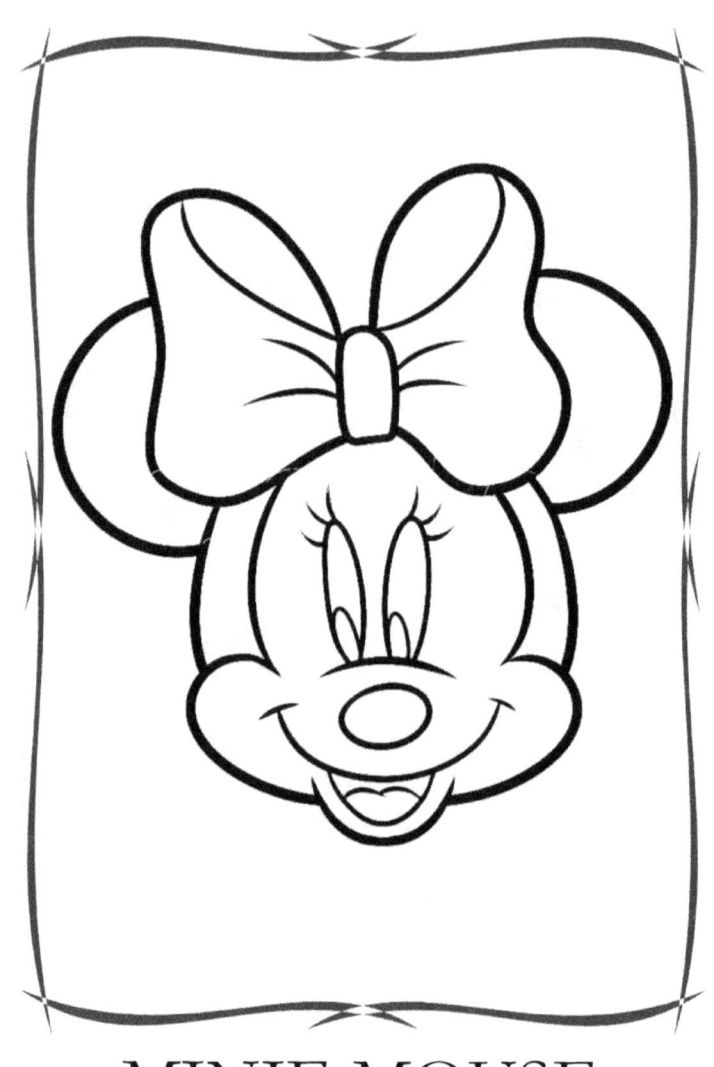

MINIE MOUSE

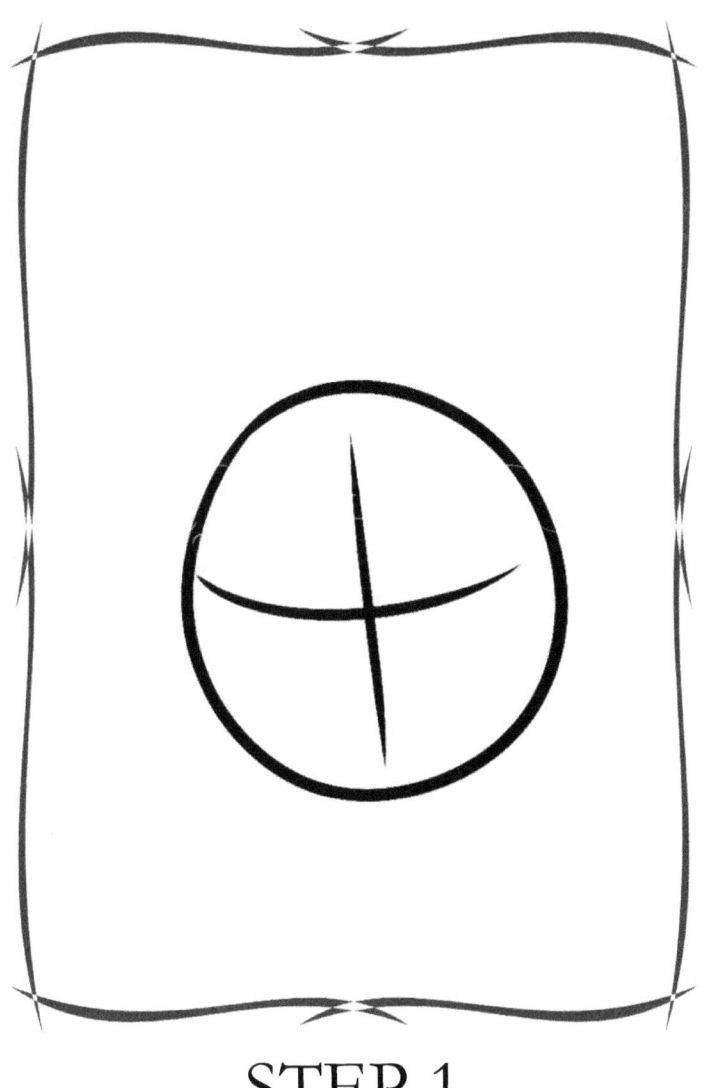

STEP 1

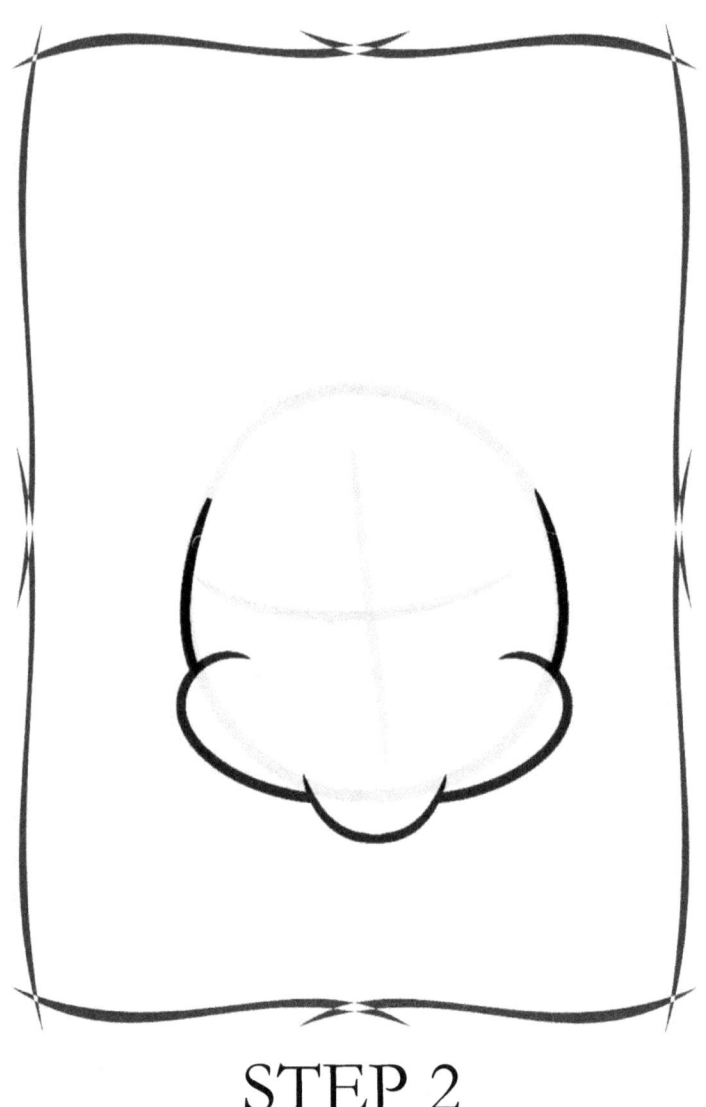

STEP 2

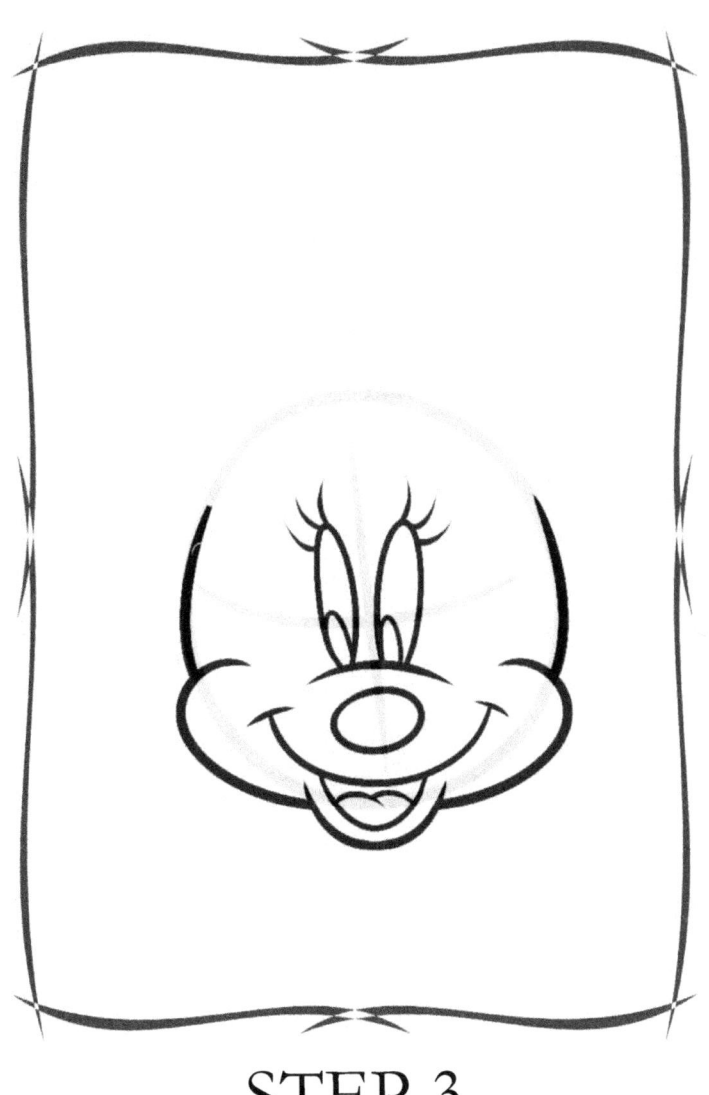

STEP 3

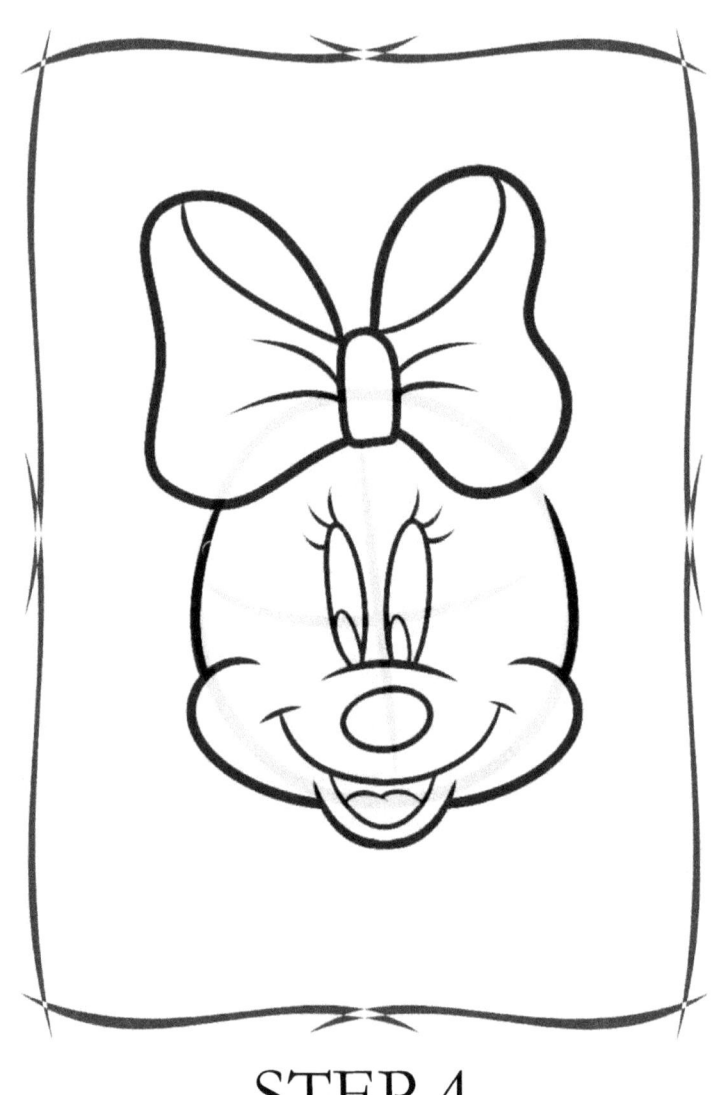

STEP 4

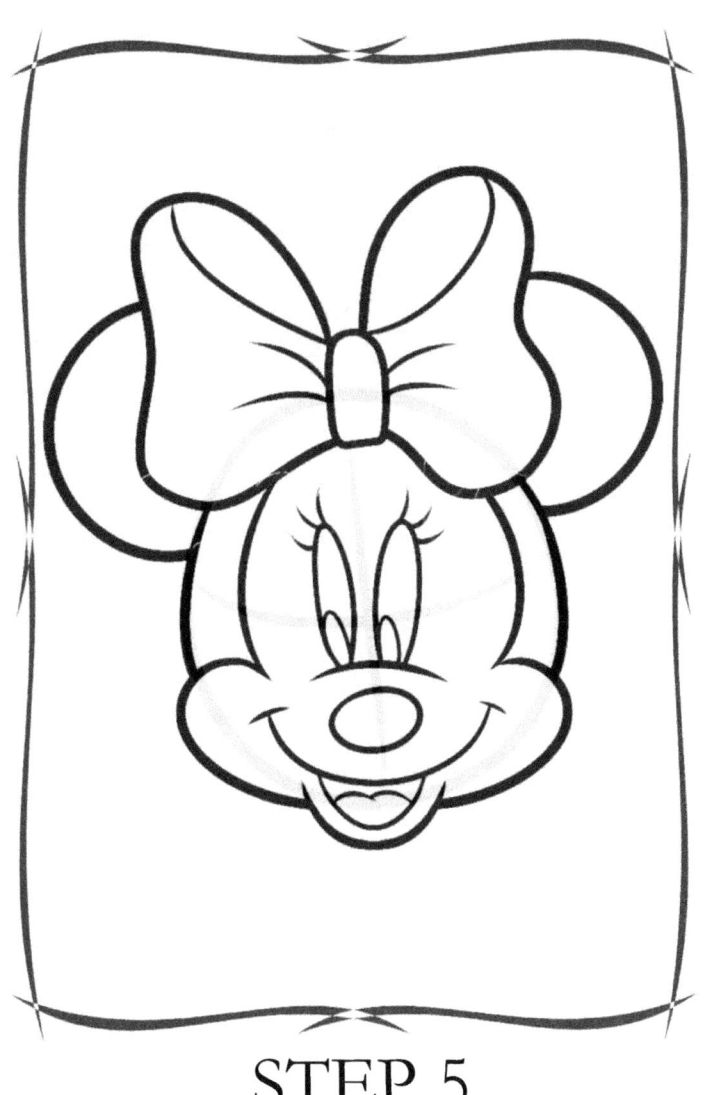

STEP 5